Edwa d F

1031 Exchanges
Made Easy
SECOND EDITION

A Comprehensive Guide to Your 1031 Exchange
Brought to You by www.1031Crowdfunding.com

IMPORTANT DISLAIMER

Table of Contents

WELCOME: 1031 EXCHANGES MADE EASY 7

PART 1: INTRODUCTION TO 1031 EXCHANGES 9

What is a 1031 Exchange? 9

History of 1031 Exchanges 9

Delayed 1031 Exchanges 10

A Delayed Exchange Timeline: 12

Reverse 1031 Exchanges.. 12

Qualified Intermediary... 13

Deadlines 15

Identification Period Deadline 15

Exchange Period Deadline... 15

Calculating Deadlines 16

Replacement Property Identification... 16

Three (3) Property Identification Rule: 17

200% of Fair Market Value Identification Rule: 17

95% Identification Rule:... 18

How to Identify Properties 20

What is Boot?..20

Types of Boot 21

Mortgage Boot 21

Cash Boot 21

Sale Proceeds 21

Excess Borrowing 21

Non-Like-Kind... 21

Personal Residence Boot 22

Offsetting Boot..22

PART 2: THE CASE FOR 1031 EXCHANGES............................23

Taking Advantage With a 1031 Exchange.......................23

Damian Mills – Case Study...26

Capital Gains or Depreciation Got You Down? 27

Capital Gains 27

Adjusted Basis...27

Cost of Sale...28

Taxation of Capital Gains 28

Depreciation 28

Calculating Depreciation 28

Taxation of Depreciation 29

Equity...29

Salvaging Equity with 1031 Exchange.........................30

Vacation Homes & 1031 Exchanges 32

Step-up in Cost Basis for Heirs 35

PART 3: DELAWARE STATUTORY TRUSTS......................37

Harold Walker – Case Study.......................................37

What is a DST? 38

Benefits of DSTs 40

7 Deadly Sins of DSTs.. 40

DSTs v. REITs v. TICs 43

REITs 43

TICs 44

Using a DST as a Backup Plan.....................................46

Diversification...48

PART 4: CONCLUSIONS..50

1031 Crowdfunding and You 51

Glossary 52

WELCOME: 1031 EXCHANGES MADE EASY

1031 Crowdfunding was founded to provide a range of quality properties for investors seeking a 1031 exchange through a Delaware Statutory Trust (DST). The 45-day Identification Period can be a very stressful event for 1031 exchange investors. 1031 Crowdfunding can ease the stress with its online turnkey solution. Our experienced team of securities and real estate professionals have created an online marketplace that can accomplish this for you within days. The headaches of dealing with the tenants, the toilets, and the trash are over!

Through our state of the art platform, you can now purchase a beneficial interest in a variety of properties across different asset classes using Delaware Statutory Trusts (DSTs). Not only does this allow you to diversify your investment dollars, but it also grants you access to larger and higher quality pieces of commercial real estate than ever before.

We spend a lot of time educating investors in the world of 1031 exchanges and DSTs. You may even be asking yourself, what is a 1031 exchange or DST? Throughout this book we will offer both basic and in-depth knowledge on these subjects and will present case studies of real scenarios many investors may encounter. The purpose of this book is to answer the questions we hear most frequently from investors and outline the 1031 exchange process in a simple, easy to understand way.

We hope you find the answers to your questions within this material, but in case you need further assistance, please give us a call at (844) 533-1031.

We Look forward to speaking with you and helping you with your 1031 exchange or DST needs.

Sincerely,

Edward Fernandez, President & CEO

PART 1: INTRODUCTION TO 1031 EXCHANGES

What is a 1031 Exchange?

Section 1031 of the Internal Revenue Code, provides a simple, strategic method for deferring capital gain or recapture tax from the sale of real property. This is done by completing what is most commonly referred to as a like-kind, or 1031 exchange. In a 1031 exchange, an owner will dispose of real property that has been held for investment or productive use in trade or business. The owner will then use the proceeds from the sale of their property to acquire a like-kind replacement property of equal or greater value. Although the process is relatively straightforward, there are concrete guidelines that must be followed to complete a fully tax-deferred exchange.

History of 1031 Exchanges

Tax-deferred exchanges have been around since 1921 as part of The Revenue Act of 1921. However, these early exchanges proved difficult by having to complete every transaction simultaneously; every transfer had to be completed on the same day to fulfill the exchange.

In the late 1970s, Starker v. United States was ruled in favor of the Starker family and established a precedent for delayed or deferred exchanges. The Starker family sold some timberland to the Crown Zellerbach Company. Instead of receiving cash on the sale, they took a credit on the books of the Crown Zellerbach. Over the course of a few years, the Starker family found properties they wished to own, and Crown Zellerbach bought the properties and applied the value of the property to the Starker's credit. Then Crown Zellerbach transferred the property deeds to the Starkers. Because the Starkers did not account for any capital gains on the timberland that was sold, and the exchange of property did not coincide with the sale of the timberland, the IRS questioned the transactions, and the case went to court. It was from this tax court conflict that led to the code change in 1984 formally recognizing the delayed exchange for the very first time. Today, the delayed exchange is the most common form of exchange we see.

Delayed 1031 Exchanges

In a delayed deferred exchange, the relinquished property is sold, and, after a delay, the replacement property is acquired.

The delayed exchange has become a popular investment model because it is a much easier than the simultaneous exchanges required of early exchangers. One of the reasons for this is that the delayed exchange offers the exchanger more freedom to complete the sale and acquisition transactions with different parties. Before delayed exchanges, simultaneous exchange transactions often required the actual swapping of deeds in order to ensure simultaneous closing of the relinquished and replacement properties. When dealing with separate buyers and sellers, the exchanger had to be extremely diligent to keep both parties and their representatives cooperating within the same timeline. The more parties involved, the greater the risk of an incomplete exchange and a receipt of a capital gains tax bill. Furthermore, delayed exchanges offer exchangers a more extensive inventory of investment options. In contrast, simultaneous exchanges that required the swapping of deeds limited the exchanger's options to properties owned by other investors who were interested in purchasing property owned by the exchanger.

While the Starker's delayed exchange spanned a period of several years, today's delayed exchange is limited to specific timeframes. The exchange period refers to the time between the closing of the relinquished property and the closing of the replacement property. Today's regulations limit the exchange period to 180 days. However, the exchange period might be shortened if the exchanger's tax return filing deadline falls before the completion of the 180 days. Regardless of when the relinquished property was sold, the replacement property must be acquired prior to the exchanger's tax return filing deadline.

In addition, today's delayed exchange must observe the identification period requirements. The identification period refers to the time between the closing of the relinquished property and the time the exchanger must identify the target properties that will serve as the replacement property for the exchange. Each exchanger has an identification period of 45 days. The identification period is the first 45 days of the 180-day exchange period. Once the identification period is over, the exchanger can only acquire from the candidate properties identified on or before the exchange period deadline or tax return filing deadline. There are allowances for investors to identify multiple candidate properties which we will get into a little later.

Forty-five days passes very quickly. To avoid disqualifying the exchange by missing the identification period deadline, exchangers must get started early. It is highly recommended that exchangers begin looking for candidate replacement properties even before the relinquished property is sold.

A Delayed Exchange Timeline:

Day 1: Closing of relinquished property

Day 2-44: Identification Period: Exchanger researches properties to acquire as replacement properties

Day 45: Deadline to identify candidate replacement properties

Day 46-179: Exchanger pursues acquisition of candidate replacement properties

Day 180: Deadline to close on the acquisition of one or more of the identified candidate properties

Reverse 1031 Exchanges

Reverse Exchange – Step One
(Park Replacement Property -- Exchange Last)

EAT holds title to Replacement Property until Relinquished Property is sold

The reverse exchange represents an exchange in which the exchanger acquires a replacement property before the actual closing of the relinquished property.

In most cases, an investor cannot sell a property and expect to identify a replacement property that he or she already owns. However, if managed carefully with extensive planning and an experienced facilitator, this kind of exchange is possible.

A reverse exchange requires an exchange accommodation titleholder (the accommodator), with the aid of a loan from the exchanger, to acquire the replacement property and warehouse, or hold, the property title until which time that the relinquished property is sold. Once the relinquished property is sold, the accommodator can accept the relinquished property's sale proceeds to finance the replacement property's acquisition. Then the replacement property title can be transferred to the exchanger along with a repayment of the loan that the exchanger had provided to the accommodator to acquire the replacement property.

Qualified Intermediary

A 1031 Exchange Qualified Intermediary (also often referred to in the real estate industry as a 1031 Exchange Accommodator or 1031 Exchange Facilitator) is a crucial part of any successful 1031 exchange transaction. The last thing you want when you think you've completed a 1031 exchange is to receive a tax bill. The truth of the matter is that the Internal Revenue Service (IRS) can invalidate 1031 exchanges and charge capital gains taxes on the sale of the relinquished property if the disposition and acquisition transactions were not completed within the 1031 exchange regulations.

To ensure a valid exchange and deferred capital gains, engage a reputable Qualified Intermediary (QI). The job of the QI is to help you navigate the complicated 1031 exchange process, helping you adequately comply with each of the exchange code's regulations and requirements. All exchange transactions, from the sale of the relinquished property to the purchase of the replacement property(ies), must be completed with the assistance of a QI.

A QI is an independent entity that is not the investor, an agent of the investor, or a related party to the investor. A QI enters into a written agreement with the investor to complete the exchange transactions on behalf of the investors to adhere to 1031 exchange requirements.

One of the primary functions of the QI is to restrict the investor's access to the sale proceeds after the sale of the relinquished property. Taxpayers are required to pay taxes on any income received in any given year. To defer paying taxes on one's income, the taxpayer must defer receipt of that income by avoiding both actual receipt and constructive receipt of that income.

Actual receipt of income is relatively uncomplicated, meaning that the taxpayer directly receives the actual income into their possession, placing it in their bank account or spending it according to their wishes. Constructive receipt, on the other hand, refers to income that is not directly paid to the taxpayer but placed under the taxpayer's control for them to access, administer or distribute as they determine.

In a delayed 1031 exchange, the category in which most exchanges fall, the sale proceeds are not directly transferred to the seller of the replacement property and must be held until the closing of a replacement property. To avoid a taxable event through actual receipt or constructive receipt of these funds, the investor cannot accept or hold the sale proceeds from the sale of the relinquished property. The Safe Harbor rules, as listed in IRS Section 1.103, require the investor to use a QI to act as an escrow holder for these funds. The ownership of the property to be sold is transferred to the QI, which then sells the property and holds the sale proceeds until the QI purchases a like-kind replacement property with the funds being held. At that time, the QI then transfers ownership of the replacement property to the investor, leaving the investor in possession of property rather than funds.

It is essential to choose a QI carefully since there is little state or federal regulation on QIs. With no licensing requirement, any agent can become a QI as long as they do not fall into one of the few categories that are restricted from acting as a QI, such as accountants, attorneys, and realtors who have served the taxpayer in their professional capacities within the prior two years, or any person or party related to the taxpayer. Furthermore, QIs often hold large sums of money on behalf of the investors they serve and often do not have a guarantee of security on those funds in the case the QI were to become bankrupt.

Before signing a contract with a QI, research and compare the services and experience of candidate companies. QIs can service exchanges under vastly differing operating procedures. For example, depending on the QI, they may make different decisions on how the funds are pooled and invested during the time in which they have possession. QIs have different fee structures. Some may charge a flat rate while others may take into consideration the interest earned on the funds during the period that the funds are held. Likewise, the interest earned on the funds may be paid to clients in various ways by different QIs. The task of choosing a reputable QI shouldn't paralyze the exchange process, but it's important to be thorough during this process.

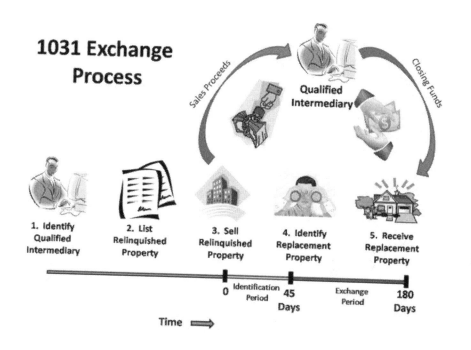

Deadlines

To properly complete a 1031 exchange, investors must meet two deadlines: the Identification Period Deadline and the Exchange Period Deadline.

Identification Period Deadline

To meet the *Identification Period Deadline*, an investor must identify a list of potential replacement properties and provide that list to their qualified intermediary at or before midnight on the 45th calendar day after the close of the relinquished property sale transaction.

Exchange Period Deadline

To meet the *Exchange Period Deadline*, the investor must complete the acquisition transaction of the replacement property(ies) on or before the earlier of 1) midnight on the 180th calendar day after the close of the relinquished property sale transaction, or 2) the due date of their Federal income tax return for the year in which the relinquished property was sold.

If your Federal income tax return for the year in which you sold the relinquished property is due before the 180-day Exchange Period deadline, then your Exchange Period deadline is the date in which your tax return is due. Instead of a 180-day Exchange Period, you will have the total number of days that exist between the close of the sale transaction on your relinquished property and the due date of your tax return.

If your tax return is due April 15th, this rule will affect you if you close on the sale transaction of a relinquished property on October 17th or any date through December 31st. If you close on these dates, then you will be required to complete your exchange on or before April 15th and will not be granted a full 180-day period to complete the transaction. However, taxpayers have the option to file for a 6-month extension on their tax returns. If exchangers facing a reduced Exchange Period file for this extension, they can maximize their Exchange Period to 180 days. It is important to note, that an extension of your tax return due date does not also allow an extension of your Exchange Period beyond the 180-days.

Calculating Deadlines

1031 exchange deadlines are based on calendar days; there are no exceptions for weekends or holidays. If the sale transaction on a relinquished property closes June 30th, July 1st becomes the first day in the countdown to the deadlines, August 14th becomes the deadline for the Identification Period, and December 27th becomes the Exchange Period deadline.

A failure to meet either of these deadlines would result in an invalid exchange, requiring the investor to pay the taxes owed on the capital gains earned by selling a relinquished property. Prepare early and know your deadlines.

Replacement Property Identification

There are very specific requirements for identifying and acquiring potential like-kind replacement properties in your 1031 exchange transaction. Section 1031 of the Internal Revenue Code ("IRC") specifies that investors must identify candidate replacement properties within a 45-day identification period in order to defer capital gains taxes through a 1031 exchange.

Because many 1031 exchange investors cannot identify with certainty their one specific replacement property within the first 45 days after the sale of their relinquished property, the IRC does provide allowances, within certain regulations, for investors to identify multiple potential replacement properties. Here is a description of the three identification rules along with an explanation of some of the reasons you might opt for one strategy over another.

Three (3) Property Identification Rule:

The Three Property Identification Rule ("Three Property Rule") states you can identify a maximum of three (3) potential like-kind replacement properties regardless of the fair market value of those properties.

The Three Property Rule is the most popular strategy by 1031 exchange investors today. If you have a reasonable assurance that you can acquire a specific property that suits your like-kind requirements, then you are likely to opt for the Three Property Rule. With this strategy, you could acquire all three of the identified like-kind replacement properties as part of your 1031 exchange, but most investors only purchase one of the three properties. The second and third identified properties merely act as 'back-up' replacement properties in case you do not or cannot acquire the first property.

200% of Fair Market Value Identification Rule:

The 200% of Fair Market Value Identification Rule ("200% Rule") states you can identify an unlimited number of like-kind replacement properties as long as the aggregate fair market value of all the identified like-kind replacement properties does not exceed 200% of the total net sales value of the relinquished property(ies) sold in your 1031 exchange.

For example, if you sold relinquished property(ies) in the amount of $2,000,000, you would be able to identify as many like-kind replacement properties as you want as long as the total fair market value of the identified like-kind replacement properties does not exceed $4,000,000 (200% of $2,000,000). The total fair market value of these identified properties is determined by the fair market value of each property at the close of your identification period, which is 45 days after the close of the sale of your relinquished property.

One reason you may opt for this strategy is if you are trying to diversify your investment portfolio and wish to acquire more than one replacement property. If you are planning to acquire four or more properties, the Three Property Rule is not sufficient for you. Or, even if you are only planning to acquire two replacement properties, it might be a good idea to have more than one 'back-up.' In this case, again, the Three Property Rule would be insufficient. Additionally, if you are unsure about your preferences for a replacement property, you can identify a handful of properties (with fair market values within the 200% allowance) and then take some extra time to decide what you really want.

Identifying more than three properties would likely provide you enough options so that at least one of them would suit your preferences and needs. Similarly, maybe your 45-day identification period is coming to a close before you have had sufficient time to research properties and make arrangements. In this case you could, again, identify a handful of properties in a hurry and then take your time determining the best option for you. There are many scenarios like these in which this strategy could benefit you.

95% Identification Rule:

The 95% Identification Exception ("95% Exception") states you can identify an unlimited number of potential like-kind replacement properties with an unlimited aggregate fair market value as long as you actually acquire and close on 95% of the value identified.

This exception can come in handy when you have attempted to identify replacement property according to the 200% Rule, but have exceeded the 200% allowance at the close of the identification period. Because the fair market value of the identified properties is determined at the close of the identification period, there are times when investors become surprised after a property's value significantly increases from the time they identified the property to the time the identification period ended. If not for the 95% Exception, the investor's exchange would be disqualified because the investor was out of compliance with the regulations of the identification period. However, in this case, the investor could still complete their exchange if they acquire at least 95% of the fair market value of the identified properties.

In other circumstances, investors may have a need to identify more than three properties and more than 200% of the sales value of the relinquished property. In these circumstances, the 95% Exception becomes necessary. It is good to have choices, but be careful with this exception. It is an exceptionally useful tool under the right circumstances but can present some tricky problems. If you do not acquire and close on at least 95% of the value of the identified like-kind replacement properties, the entire 1031 exchange transaction will be disallowed.

Things to Note:

- If investors identify more properties than allowed by the Three Property Rule or the 200% Rule and cannot apply the 95% Exception, it will be as if no properties were identified.

- If investors do not identify properties within the 45-day identification period, the 1031 exchange becomes disqualified.

- Identified properties must be acquired before the exchange period deadline, 180 days following the close of the sale of the relinquished property, in order to qualify as replacement properties in the 1031 exchange.

- Properties not included on the list of identified replacement properties will not be considered valid replacement properties to satisfy the requirements of the 1031 exchange.

- If an identified property is acquired before the close of the identification period, neither that property nor its fair market value will be considered when determining the total number of identified properties or the aggregate fair market value of the identified properties. (It will still qualify as a replacement property for purposes of the 1031 exchange.)

- Therefore, if an identified property is acquired prior to the close of the identification period, the investor can still identify three other properties in adherence to the Three Property Rule or multiple other properties with aggregate values up to 200%. Likewise, if an investor is planning to acquire 95% of the aggregate fair market value of the identified properties, the value of the property acquired within the identification period will not be included in the aggregate fair market value of which needs to be acquired or the aggregate value of properties acquired in order to meet the 95%.

How to Identify Properties

Replacement properties that you are considering for acquisition in your 1031 exchange should be identified to your QI and must be identified no later than midnight of the 45th calendar day following the close of your relinquished property sale transaction.

To identify potential replacement properties to your QI, you must provide a written and signed document that unambiguously describes the properties you wish to identify. The property description may include a legal description, street address, or distinguishable name.

If in the case you wish to revoke the identification of a candidate replacement property, you must also provide a written and signed document that unambiguously describes the property that you wish to remove from the list of identified properties.

What is Boot?

'Boot' is an old English term that means "Something given in addition to." In a 1031 exchange, boot is a common term for additional value received when acquiring a replacement property in a 1031 exchange. It is important to understand what items will be considered additional value, or boot, because boot will cause a taxable event.

The IRS code requires that a like-kind property must be acquired to replace a relinquished property. Boot typically encompasses items in a sale that are not like-kind.

A rule of thumb to remember to avoid a tax bill is to trade across or up, never down. In other words, the amount of the mortgage you take out to finance your replacement property should always be equal to or greater than the amount owed on the relinquished property. The amount of equity held on the replacement property should always be equal to or greater than the amount of equity held on the relinquished property. If this rule is followed, then you are likely to avoid being taxed on additional value gained by using funds from the sale of the relinquished property to purchase non like-kind property, finance services or pad your bank account.

(844) 533-1031

Types of Boot

Mortgage Boot or **Debt Reduction Boot** occurs when the debt owed on the replacement property is less than the debt that was owed on the relinquished property. Reducing your debt liability is considered income because it is cash that you once owed that will now remain in your pocket at the time the debt matures. Income, as you know, is taxable.

Cash Boot occurs in several ways. One of the most obvious ways you can acquire cash boot is to have a net cash received amount. When the cash received from the sale of the relinquished property is greater than the cash paid to purchase the replacement property, you will have a net cash received amount that will be considered income, and, again, income is taxable. Another way you can accumulate cash boot is to have a promissory note incorporated into the exchange. Cash boot would also include the use of interest earned on the sale proceeds while they were held before being used in the acquisition of the replacement property. Furthermore, in some cases the seller of the replacement property may pay for repairs that you, as the buyer, have required. The value of these repairs will also be considered cash boot.

Sale Proceeds can result as boot if they are used to pay non-qualified expenses, such as service costs at closing that are not considered closing costs. Such services could include rent proration's, utility escrow charges, tenant damage deposits transferred to the buyer, and any other charges unrelated to the closing. To avoid turning your sale proceeds into boot, pay for such items using cash out of your pocket.

Excess Borrowing can result as boot if you borrow more money than you need to purchase the replacement property. If the loan amount is too great, you will not be able to use all of your exchange funds to purchase the replacement property and will be taxed on any funds remaining.

Non-Like-Kind or **Personal Property Boot** occurs when the purchase of a replacement property includes non-like-kind or personal property items. This is a less common form of boot, but it is important to know that items such as appliances, furniture, farm sprinkler equipment, fixtures, etc. are considered personal property rather than like-kind. If the replacement property purchase includes personal items, the value of the like-kind property alone is less than the purchase price for the like-kind property in addition to the personal property items. You will be taxed on the value of the personal property items obtained with the replacement property if the like-kind property on its own is not of equal or greater value than the relinquished property. The best way to avoid personal property boot is to clearly state in the selling contract that the listed personal property items are excluded from the sale. You can purchase these items separately with a separate sale agreement, using cash out of your pocket rather than cash received from the sale of the relinquished property.

Personal Residence Boot is another less common form of boot that occurs when you choose to use a part of the replacement property as a personal residence. For example, if you acquire a property with multiple units, you cannot live in one of them. You will be taxed on the value of the portion of the property in which you choose to reside if the value of the remainder of the property is not equal to or greater than the value of the relinquished property.

Be sure to discuss all items included in the sale of your relinquished property and the acquisition of your replacement property with your QI. Your QI should be your source to help ensure you have not accumulated any of these forms of boot whether intentionally or inadvertently.

Offsetting Boot

Boot received can be offset by boot paid. Only your net boot will be taxable, so even if you do encounter boot in your transactions, you may be able to offset it and complete a totally tax-deferred transaction. It is best to consult your QI to determine how to offset boot received, but here are a few general rules:

- Cash boot paid will offset cash boot received. However, take note that cash boot paid can only offset cash boot received when both forms of boot occur at the same closing table. In other words, cash boot paid at the relinquished property closing will not offset cash boot received at the replacement property closing.

- Debt incurred on the replacement property can offset debt-reduction boot received on the relinquished property.

- Cash boot paid can offset debt-reduction boot received.

- Debt boot paid will never offset cash boot received.

- Exchange expenses, such as transaction and closing costs paid, can offset net cash boot received.

(844) 533-1031

PART 2: THE CASE FOR 1031 EXCHANGES

Taking Advantage With a 1031 Exchange

Selling an asset for significantly more than you paid to acquire it always brings gratification. You've made a good investment and earned the reward. You probably have plenty of ideas for how you'd like to use it: save it, get out of debt, pay for that item that has so far been out of your financial reach, reinvest it to increase it, etc. Oh so many options...

You might not want to get too carried away too quickly. Much of that income will soon be used to pay the taxes you've incurred on the appreciation of your asset. You can still save it, spend it or reinvest it; but expect to save, spend or reinvest only a portion of the total amount earned from your sale. This is the inevitable case with most investments. However, if you are in a position to complete a 1031 exchange, it doesn't have to be your inevitability.

By completing a 1031 exchange, you can defer capital gains taxes incurred on the sale of a relinquished property and reinvest the entire sale amount into a replacement property. Deferring the payment of taxes allows you to keep those funds on your balance sheet, working to continue building your wealth. Likewise, deferring the payment of taxes means you have a larger reinvestment amount that will yield higher returns than reinvesting what would be left over after paying capital gains taxes.

	Sale Example		Exchange Example	
Sale Price	$	350,000	$	350,000
Closing Costs	$	(25,000)	$	(25,000)
Maximum Federal Gains Tax of 20%	$	(70,000)	$	-
Proceeds Available for Reinvestment	$	255,000	$	325,000
Potential Annual Cash Flow	$	17,850	$	22,750
Yield on Un-Taxed Proceeds		Equivalent: 5.49%		7.00%
Yield on Taxed Proceeds		7.00%		Equivalent: 8.92%

Here's what you should notice:

- The sale price is the same in both examples.

- The potential annual cash flow after reinvesting is significantly higher in the exchange example.

- The investor in the sale example would have to reinvest in a like-kind property paying a 8.92% annual yield in order to earn an equivalent $22,750 annual cash flow on the reinvestment of the $255,000 sale proceeds.

- The investor in the sale example is only receiving the equivalent of a 5.49% annual yield on their highest potential reinvestment amount had they deferred taxes like the investor in the exchange example.

- Whether you look at the potential income of the investor in the sale example or the equivalent percentage of annual returns this investor will make in comparison to the investor in the exchange example, it is clear that the investor in the exchange example has the advantage to build wealth more efficiently.

- Furthermore, with nearly $100,000 more to acquire real estate, the investor in the exchange example has a greater opportunity to purchase a higher quality property that may yield higher returns than what the investor in the sale example could afford. The investor in the sale example does have the option to acquire a loan to purchase the same property as the investor in the exchange example, but much of the annual cash flow would be used to pay the loan fees, reducing the net cash flow to the investor. Why borrow cash when you can defer taxes and use your own cash to fund your investment?

(844) 533-1031

- Finally, consider how the potential annual cash flow can increase each time the investor in the exchange example exchanges property through a 1031 exchange. With each exchange, this investor defers the payment of taxes on their capital gains and increases the proceeds they have available for reinvestment. For example, after the next exchange, the investor may have $350,000 of available proceeds for reinvesting. Then some years later, after another exchange, the investor may have $375,000 of available proceeds for reinvesting. If the investor continues to invest in like-kind properties paying 7% annual returns, the annual cash flow increases with each increase in the reinvested amounts.

1031 exchange investors have the potential to build greater wealth because they take advantage of tax-deferred opportunities and leverage their own income to achieve higher returns on their reinvestments.

Damian Mills – Case Study

Damian Mills spent the morning looking over his finances. After receiving the final divorce settlement papers last month, Damian decided it was time to figure out how he was going to salvage his remaining assets and set himself up to rebuild his portfolio. Damian stared out the window of the apartment he had moved into temporarily while he awaited the settlement. He wasn't looking forward to the business at hand but decided it was necessary.

First things first, where was he going to live? He wanted out of this apartment as soon as possible. While his ex-wife received the title to the house they had shared, he got to keep the mountain home he had bought for her when they were first married. She was from a small town in the Rocky Mountains. Having moved to the city to be with him, she struggled with culture shock and homesickness. Still wooing his new bride, he thought a vacation home in the mountains would be a special get-away location for the two of them and a nice retreat for her when city life became too much. It was...for a while.

Taking permanent residence in the mountain house was out of the question; he couldn't commute to work from there. Besides, in his mind, it was hers. He would never enjoy it again without her. He could continue to rent it out for income, but even the constant reminder of it would be too painful. The house would have to be sold.

Damian began running the numbers. He knew the house had appreciated, so he figured there would be a good chance for a nice profit. However, after doing a basic calculation, he realized that once he repaid the loan and paid capital gain taxes his net profit would result in only about $27,000. Though this amount could be the basis for rebuilding his portfolio, it was not an amount that encouraged optimism and was a $13,000 loss of his original down payment. How was this possible? Damian began to research his situation.

(844) 533-1031

Capital Gains or Depreciation Got You Down?

Are capital gains taxes or depreciation recapture forcing you to take a loss on the sale of a property you should have profited from? You're probably aware that capital gains taxes and depreciation recapture will be owed on any profit made from the sale of a property but probably didn't expect those taxes to cause you to lose a portion of your original investment. How did you end up here? To answer that question, we must first understand capital gains, depreciation, and equity.

Capital Gains

To be clear, capital gains are not:

The amount the property is sold for,

The amount of cash you put in your pocket after the sale,

The difference between the appraisal amount and the sale amount,

The amount remaining after loans are paid off, or

The difference between the purchase price and the sale price.

Instead capital gains are the profits earned after subtracting the adjusted basis and the cost of sale from the property's sale price,

Sales Price - Adjusted Basis - Cost of Sale = **Capital Gain**

Adjusted Basis

Your adjusted basis or cost basis is going to be informed by calculations starting with the purchase price you paid when you bought the property. Your purchase price is the starting amount of your cost basis, which actually changed over time.

For instance, if you made any improvements to the property, that amount should be added. Likewise, if you deducted any depreciation while you owned that property, that should be subtracted. Therefore, to find your final adjusted basis, take the original purchase price plus any improvements and less any depreciation.

Original Purchase Price + Improvements - Depreciation = **Net Adjusted Basis**

Cost of Sale

Every sale has a cost to it. There are closing costs, such as the fees charged by the real estate agents, to any real estate transaction that will reduce the seller's profits. Any of such qualifying closing costs can be deducted from the sales price before determining the seller's taxable capital gains.

Taxation of Capital Gains

Depending on the short-term or long-term nature of your investment in the property and whether or not self-employment taxes will factor in, you could be taxed as low as 15% on your capital gains or as high as 40%. The time that you owned the property is not the only factor that determines whether you will be taxed at long-term or short-term rates.

Depreciation

Depreciation as an annual income tax deduction that allows investors to recover the cost or other basis of certain property over the time the property is used. It is an allowance for the wear and tear, deterioration, or obsolescence of the property.

For real estate, depreciation is the calculation of loss of value on any improvements to a property. In most cases, land, as the basis of a property's value, will not endure loss in value through wear and tear. Therefore, the value of the land doesn't usually factor into a depreciation calculation. The buildings that are constructed on the land become the improvements eligible for depreciation deductions.

Calculating Depreciation

When it comes to the basic calculation for your depreciation deduction of real estate, we must consider how long the property has been determined to last. Rather than deducting the actual costs incurred by wear and tear on the property each year, deductions are averaged over the valuable life of the property. Most commercial real estate improvements are presumed to last 39 years while residential property improvements are presumed to last 27.5 years. Depreciation considers the cost basis of the depreciation-eligible portion of the property and divides that amount by the established valuable lifespan of the property to determine the annual deductible amount.

(844) 533-1031

Cost Basis / Valuable lifespan = **Annual Depreciation Deduction**

Depreciation deductions may differ for the first year if the property was not in service the entire year and may change in later years if a significant change in cost basis or lifespan occurs.

Taxation of Depreciation

Annual depreciation deductions will increase to the property investor's annual cash flow.

When property is depreciated on a tax return and deductions are taken from the income earned on that property, the investor will owe fewer taxes to the IRS. A property may have a $12,000 annual pre-tax net cash flow but then will owe the IRS income taxes on that $12,000. If a property is depreciated, the tax return will deduct the depreciation deduction from that $12,000 income, and the amount owed to the IRS will be reduced. This allows a greater portion of that $12,000 to remain in the investor's pocket, resulting in an increased after-tax net cash flow.
While depreciation can increase an investor's annual cash flow, it can cause a significant reduction to the investor's profits when the property is sold.

Depreciation deductions will be recaptured by the IRS when the sales price exceeds the adjusted cost basis of a property. If an investor depreciated a property by $50,000 over the time of ownership and reduced a property's cost basis from $300,000 to $250,000 and then sells the property for $290,000, the investor will owe the IRS a significant percentage in depreciation recapture of that $40,000 difference.

Depreciation is a complex tax deduction with many varying factors that will affect investors. To fully understand depreciation, including how the year the property was purchased and depreciation methods factor into depreciation calculations, it is important to consult a tax advisor or IRS publication 946.

Equity

Equity represents the hard-earned value that is in any property. To determine one's equity, take the gross selling price and subtract the closing costs, then further subtract the amount of any remaining debt. The remaining amount will be the equity in that property.

Selling Price - Cost of Sale - Debt = **Equity**

The amount of equity an investor has in a property will affect the ultimate profits the investor can earn on that property. If an investor has a high loan-to-value ratio, the equity percentage is going to be low. When equity in a property is low and capital gains are high, investors can find themselves with little remaining cash after repaying loans and paying capital gains taxes and depreciation recapture. It is even possible to owe so much on a property in mortgage loans that the investor doesn't even receive enough cash from the sale to repay the loan and pay the taxes.

Salvaging Equity with 1031 Exchange

Investors who are experiencing a fleeting joy because loans and taxes are eliminating the profits they had anticipated from a large appreciation of the value of their property may want to consider the option of a 1031 exchange. When the investor reinvests the entire value of the property that was sold into a new investment property through a 1031 exchange, the payment of the capital gains taxes and depreciation recapture can be deferred. Instead of paying taxes and starting from a reduced equity amount, the investor can keep their entire equity and make a new investment equal in value to the prior investment.

After reading this article, Damian realized his problem was precisely due to a significant appreciation of his mountain home's value and a high loan-to-value ratio.

He had purchased the home for $200,000,

Paid an additional $10,000 in closing costs,

Put 40% down for an $80,000 down payment, and

Took a $130,000 loan to finance the remainder of the purchase costs.

Over time the mountain property had appreciated, so Damian and his wife decided to refinance the mountain house in order to have additional cash to purchase a permanent residence.

With an appraised value on the mountain home of $300,000, Damian increased his loan to value amount to 80% and increased the loan amount to $240,000.

Based on his knowledge of the local real estate, Damian figured he could sell the house for about $320,000 but would lose about $22,400 (about 7% of the sales price) in closing costs. After repaying the loan, he'd have a net sales profit of $57,600. This was an amount he could use as a basis for

(844) 533-1031

the rebuilding of his portfolio, but he knew he had to consider capital gains taxes.

First, he determined his cost basis.

Purchase price: $200,000

+ Closing costs: $10,000

+ Improvements: $0

- Depreciation: $0

= Cost basis: $210,000

Then he determined the capital gains.

Sales price: $320,000

- Closing costs: $22,400

- Cost basis: $210,000

= Capital gains: $87,600

Damian knew his tax bracket causes him to pay about 35% on earned income. With gains of $87,600, he would be paying about $30,660, leaving him a net earned income of only $26,940 to reinvest.

As he re-read the article, Damien wondered if he could find a way to make his property eligible for a 1031 exchange. If he could defer the capital gains taxes, he could have a much higher starting point for the rebuilding of his portfolio. Damian needed to know more about 1031 exchanges.

Vacation Homes & 1031 Exchanges

Do you have a vacation or second home that doesn't get used very often anymore? Have you considered replacing that home with something new?

Or perhaps, have you considered converting the equity in that home into investment funds? If you've thought about selling that vacation or second home, have you wished you could sell it without having to pay high capital gain taxes?

Maybe you don't yet own a vacation or second home, but would one day like to. Have you considered investing in exchangeable real estate that will help you earn the funds to purchase a vacation or second home through a 1031 exchange?

If so, you're in luck. Since March 10, 2008, rules on exchanging vacation and second homes have become much clearer, making it possible to complete a tax-deferred 1031 exchange of a vacation or second home for a replacement vacation or second home when certain guidelines are followed.

Revenue Procedure 2008-16 provided the guidelines that make it possible to complete a 1031 exchange of vacation and second homes.

The guidelines state a vacation or second home can qualify as the relinquished property in a 1031 exchange if:

- The subject property has been owned and held by the investor for at least 24 months immediately preceding the 1031 Exchange ("qualifying use period"); and

- The subject property was rented at fair market rental rates to other people for at least 14 days (or more) during each of the preceding two years; and

- The investor limited his or her personal use and enjoyment of the property to not more than 14 days during each of the preceding two years, or ten percent of the number of days that the subject property was actually rented out to other people during each of the preceding two years.

(844) 533-1031

Likewise, a vacation or second home can qualify as the replacement property in a 1031 exchange if:

- The subject property is owned and held by the investor for at least 24 months immediately following the 1031 Exchange ("qualifying use period"); and

- The subject property was rented at fair market rental rates to other people for at least 14 days (or more) during each of the following two years; and

- The investor limits his or her personal use and enjoyment of the property to not more than 14 days during each of the following two years, or ten percent of the number of days that the subject property was actually rented out to other people during each of the following two years.

While these guidelines do help us understand how a vacation or second home can be considered an investment property in order to qualify under 1031 exchange regulations, there are circumstances that do not fall within these guidelines that may still qualify your vacation or second home as an eligible property for a 1031 exchange. Don't miss an opportunity because you don't fall perfectly within the mold, discuss your specific circumstances with your legal and tax advisors to see if your vacation or second home can qualify as an eligible relinquished or replacement property in a tax deferred exchange.

Some property owners interested in completing a 1031 exchange of vacation or second homes may feel these guidelines restrict them from determining the use of the properties they own. The fact is that 1031 exchanges were established to make tax allowances for investors and business owners to more easily do business. But who says you shouldn't be able to enjoy a property purchased as an investment? That's one of the reasons to be a bit grateful that these guidelines have been stated. We now know that personal property simply has to be converted into property that is also used for investment or business in order to qualify as an exchangeable property. Prior to 2008 and the guidelines of Revenue Procedure 2008-16, it was hard to determine whether or not a property used as a vacation or second home could be exchanged at all.

Here's a little history for your reference. The confusion occurred because in 1981 Private Letter Ruling 198103117 was issued by the Internal Revenue Service, indicating that properties that were, at least partially, used for investment or business purposes could be exchanged. Then in 1991, the Department of the Treasury issued the Deferred Exchange Regulations that indicated only properties held solely for investment or business could be exchanged. It wasn't until 2007 when Tax Court

Memorandum 2007-134 was filed and clarified that as long as the primary intent for the property was investment or business, the property could also have personal uses.

The hard part was determining how to prove primary intent. Since the guidelines of Revenue Procedure 2008-16 were published, we can know for how long and how a property must be used in order establish its' eligibility for a tax-deferred exchange without having to define the owner's intent for the property.

Depending on the numbers and your personal circumstances, jumping through hoops to make your vacation or second home fall within these guidelines, may or may not be worth it to you. But at least you now know it's possible to sell or acquire a vacation or second home through a tax-deferred exchange that would allow those capital gains to increase your investment capabilities.

Step-up in Cost Basis for Heirs

Leave your heirs with assets, not liabilities. As some say it, the way to get the most out of 1031 exchanging is to "swap 'till you drop."

Swap...

When investors continue the cycle of swapping real estate indefinitely, they continue to defer the payment of the capital gains taxes indefinitely. The longer investors keep their equity invested in real estate and defer taxes, the greater their opportunities are to increase their wealth at exponentially faster rates.

Drop...

The deferred taxes would become owed if ever the investor sold the real estate without reinvesting the gains into replacement real estate, BUT if the investor continues to own the exchanged real estate until the time he or she passes away (or drops, as the saying goes), the deferred tax liability is not transferred to the heirs with the real estate.

Step-up basis for heirs

When the real estate is transferred to the investor's heirs, the heirs receive a step-up in cost basis equal to the fair market value of the property at the time the investor passed away. The heirs do not inherit any depreciation recapture or capital gains tax liabilities on the real estate.

Often investors add a family member to the title of a property, unknowingly gifting the property to that family member and breaking the chain of events that would give their heirs the step-up in cost basis.

In many cases, holding assets in joint ownership with one's beneficiaries may be the easiest way to transfer the assets after the primary owner becomes deceased. However, as long as the property has a living owner, be it the original exchanger or a joint owner, that owner is responsible for the tax liability on the property. In order to eliminate the accumulated capital gains taxes owed on real estate that has been acquired through a 1031 exchange, the real estate must pass to the heir after the owner has passed away.

For example:

On the date of his death, a father owned a piece of real estate with a fair market value of $500,000. The property was purchased for $200,000. The daughter received the property through the father's will. Because the daughter received the property with a step-up in cost basis equal to the fair market value, her cost basis is $500,000. If the daughter chose to immediately sell the property for $500,000, she would not have earned any capital gains or incurred any capital gains taxes. If she held the property for some time and later sold the property, she would only recognize gain for the amount greater than her original $500,000.

Therefore, if she sold the property for $600,000, she would owe capital gains taxes on the $100,000 gain. However, the daughter could consider the option to defer the capital gains taxes incurred as a result of this sale and complete a 1031 exchange by replacing the inherited property for like-kind real estate.

The father's purchase price, date of purchase, and exchange history become irrelevant to taxation of the real estate once it is in the daughter's possession. *It is worth it to note that the fair market value of the real estate will be included in the father's estate and may be subject to federal and/or state estate taxes.

"Swapping 'till you drop" can make the most of leveraging your income. 1031 exchanging enables you to leave your heirs with assets, offering an opportunity to continue building wealth and deferring tax liabilities.

PART 3: DELAWARE STATUTORY TRUSTS

Harold Walker – Case Study

The phone rang. Harold looked at the caller ID and saw that it was the tenant in unit B of the investment duplex he owned and managed. What could he want now? Harold wondered as he hesitated to answer the phone. Harold Walker had worked as a civil engineer for over 30 years. He bought the duplex 15 years into his career as a retirement plan. He was told the income from the investment would increase his retirement savings and then provide a continual income to live on once he retired. After 20 years of managing the property and a cycle of tenants making one repair request after another, Harold had become fairly disinterested in the property. The constant reminder from his wife about the investment benefits was the only thing that persuaded Harold to answer the phone.

Later that day, Harold was talking to a buddy of his, David, about the investment property. David was one of the reasons Harold bought the property in the first place. David had spent most of his career owning, managing and exchanging real estate. Harold wondered how David hadn't burnt out on real estate years ago. As it turned out, Harold was surprised to find out that David had burned out, and hadn't actively managed property in about five years.

When David decided he was ready to enjoy retirement, he hired a company to take over the management of his investment properties. He figured he could still enjoy the residual income, without dealing with the headaches associated with actively managing his property. Then he found out about Delaware Statutory Trusts (DSTs), an option that also allowed him residual income without active management, but also offered many other benefits of higher income potential and a simple purchase/1031 exchange process. He had since exchanged each of his individually owned properties for partial ownership in multiple properties owned through DSTs. Now all David worried about was

collecting his income checks from the mail and considering what DST he would exchange into when one of the current DST properties sells.
Harold couldn't believe what he was hearing. Why had he been left to suffer the stress of property management when he was ready to retire? He had to know more about DSTs.

What is a DST?

DST stands for Delaware Statutory Trust. A Delaware Statutory Trust is a separate legal entity created as a trust under Delaware statutory law. While the concept of business trusts, especially those that involved the holding of real property, dates back as early as 16th century English Common Law, DSTs gained legal recognition with the passage of the Delaware Statutory Trust Act in 1988 (12 Del. C. 3801 et. Seq.,). Under the act, developed on the premise of trust law, statutory trusts became recognized as their own legal entity, separate from their trustee(s), offering freedom from the corporate law template. Within the tradition of trust law, freedom of contract allows the trustee(s) to structure their entity in a way that is most beneficial to the relationship of all parties and their expertise, while offering liability protection similar to that of a limited liability company or partnership.

A Delaware Statutory Trust is in the nature of a unit investment trust or a fixed investment trust. The trust acquires and maintains assets such as securities, real estate, etc. Investors then have an opportunity to purchase units of beneficial interests in the trust, thereby becoming beneficiaries of the trust's assets. Because the trust is not considered a taxable entity, all the profits, losses, etc. are passed through directly to the beneficiaries. This type of trust offers a vehicle for investors to have interests in certain assets without having to hold the title to or manage those assets.

For the purpose of completing a 1031 exchange, IRS Revenue Ruling 2004-86 opened the way for eligible DST investments to qualify as the replacement property in a 1031 exchange. This revenue ruling states that a beneficial interest in a DST that owned real estate can be considered a "direct interest in real estate." As a result, owning interest in a DST that owns real estate equates, in the eyes of the IRS, to holding title on real estate. Because of this ruling, DSTs have become the most common ownership structure used by smaller investors to own investment-grade real estate together with other investors.

Who's responsible?

When investing in a DST, investors purchase units of beneficial interest and become beneficiaries of the DST's operations. As beneficiaries, investors have the following rights and responsibilities:

- Have the right to receive distributions. Based on the investors' pro rata interests in the trust, they have the right to receive distributions from the operations of the trust, either from rental income or from the eventual sale of the property. As with any business, operations can result in profits or losses; therefore, distributions are not guaranteed.

- Do not have the responsibility of property management. DSTs are operated and managed by trustees, removing any responsibility or right for the beneficiaries to participate in the day-to-day handling of the property's operation or the timing and details of the eventual sale of the property.

- Are not liable for the property. Investors do not have deeded title to the property; therefore, they are not liable for the property.

- Incur tax responsibility. Since the trust is not considered a taxable entity, all the profits, losses, etc. are passed through directly to the beneficiaries.

Now let's take a look at the responsibilities of the trustee who operates and manages the DST. Because the trust itself holds the deed to the property, the trustee's liability for the property is limited. The trustee has the responsibility to make decisions:

- On behalf of the trust,

- For the benefit of the beneficiaries,

- Regarding day to day operations,

- Regarding timing and arrangements for the sale of the trust's asset, and

- Adhering to IRS Ruling 2004-86, which names the seven deadly sins that limit the DST's trustee's power.

Benefits of DSTs

7 Deadly Sins of DSTs

The Internal Revenue Ruling 2004-86 names seven deadly sins that limit the DST trustee's power. Deadly sins can sound intimidating, and perhaps it should be for DST trustees. Engaging in any one of these prohibited acts can have serious consequences for the DST and its beneficiaries. However, when obeyed, these regulations provide additional protection and benefit to the beneficiaries by ensuring the trustee distributes funds properly to beneficiaries and does not take unnecessary risks with the DST's assets.

Below is a list of the seven deadly sins outlined by the ruling along with an explanation of how they can help the investor.

1. **Once the offering is closed, there can be no future equity contribution to the DST by either current or new co-investors or beneficiaries.**

When investors purchase shares of beneficial interest in a DST, they purchase a percentage of ownership in the DST. If a trustee decided to accept additional contributions to the DST after the offering closed, the original investors' ownership percentages would be diluted, decreasing their claim to the DST's assets. While there are times a fund and its investors may benefit from additional contributions that can be used to help a struggling fund, the risk of additional losses is often greater than the likelihood that the increased investment will turn the struggling fund into a profitable fund.

2. **The Trustee of the DST cannot renegotiate the terms of the existing loans, nor can it borrow any new funds from any other lender or party.**

Loans are liabilities. When an investor purchases shares of beneficial interest in a DST, the loan amounts are disclosed. Part of the due diligence an investor completes before purchasing shares of any fund is to understand its liabilities and decide whether or not they believe the liabilities are within reason. If a trustee is allowed to take risks and assume greater liabilities, they do so without the consent of the beneficiaries and possibly to the dissatisfaction of the beneficiaries. Since DST beneficiaries do not have the right to vote on operating decisions, the ruling prevents some actions (such as assuming debt) that can have a significant effect on the beneficiaries' interests. Additionally, as stated above, more money invested into a fund can help a struggling fund, but it can also be a risk of greater losses.

3. The Trustee cannot reinvest the proceeds from the sale of its investment real estate.

The ruling requires that all proceeds earned by the DST must be distributed to the beneficiaries rather than be reinvested. By prohibiting a trustee from deciding to reinvest proceeds on behalf of the DST's beneficiaries, the IRS ensures that beneficiaries have the right to determine how and when to reinvest or use the capital earned from their investment in the DST. Often once the assets of a DST are sold, the DST sponsor will create a new DST offering, giving beneficiaries the option to reinvest their capital with the sponsor. The investor also has the ability to find a separate investment opportunity or cash out as their own circumstances may dictate.

4. The Trustee is limited to making capital expenditures with respect to the property to those for a) normal repair and maintenance, (b) minor non-structural capital improvements, and (c) those required by law.

This deadly sin permits trustees to reasonably maintain the real estate property and its value, but it restricts the trustee from risking the beneficiaries' investments to upgrade the property when there can be no assurance that the cost of the upgrade will be recouped and increased at the time of sale.

5. Any liquid cash held in the DST between distribution dates can only be invested in short-term debt obligations.

An investment in a short-term debt obligation is considered a cash equivalent because it is readily converted back into cash that can be distributed to beneficiaries at the distribution time. Because of the short-term nature of such an investment, there is little risk of change in the value. Allowance of this kind of investment gives the trustee the ability to continue to increase the value of the fund on behalf of the investors without risk of causing significant detriment to the fund's value.

6. All cash, other than necessary reserves, must be distributed to the co-investors or beneficiaries on a current basis.

DSTs are permitted to keep cash reserves so that they are prepared in the event the property requires repair or faces unexpected expenses. However, they are required to distribute earnings and proceeds to the beneficiaries within the expected timeframe. This prevents the trustee from having the ability to spend or invest the funds outside of allowable expenditures. It also protects the beneficiaries' rights to receive their income in a timely manner so they may use it as they choose rather than having it locked into the fund any longer than it should be.

7. The Trustee cannot enter into new leases or renegotiate the current leases.

Because of this deadly sin, DSTs operate best when they have invested in properties with long-term leases to creditworthy tenants on a triple-net basis or with a master-lease structure to hold multifamily, student and senior housing, hospitality, and self-storage facilities. These types of leases provide a more secure investment in contrast to riskier year by year multi-tenant contracts that can leave properties with vacancies and less than optimal operating levels. By forcing trustees into secure leases, beneficiaries can be assured that trustees will not make risky leasing decisions. The ruling does allow for exceptions to be made in the case of a tenant bankruptcy or insolvency.

These seven deadly sins are in place as part of the regulations that allow DSTs to qualify as suitable investments for the purpose of a tax-deferred 1031 exchange. As described above, they have their benefits for investors, but at times can cause challenges for trustees with even the purest of intentions. In the unfortunate event that a DST finds itself in danger of losing a property because the seven deadly sins have prohibited the trustee from taking the necessary actions to remedy a problem, the state of Delaware permits the DST to convert to a Limited Liability Company ("LLC") if a provision was listed in the origination documents.

Like a DST, this Springing LLC, as it is called, contains bankruptcy remote protections for the lender and the beneficiaries. However, unlike the DST, the LLC is not restricted by the seven deadly sins, giving the trustee, now the LLC manager, the ability to raise funds or renegotiate leases as necessary to protect the property and the fund. While such a conversion can have considerable tax implications for investors because LLCs do not qualify to defer capital gains taxes through 1031 exchanges, converting to an LLC can rescue a DST in danger and prevent heavy losses by the beneficiaries.

DSTs v. REITs v. TICs

REITs

Real Estate Investment Trusts, or REITs, have attracted many investors who want to benefit from real estate investments but do not want the personal liability or management responsibilities. Therefore, as we discuss real estate investing, it is necessary to mention REITs. Like DSTs, a REIT, is a type of investment trust that owns real estate, offers shares of stock to investors, and distributes all of its net operating income to stockholders.

In contrast, REITs operate from a different set of regulations and requirements than DSTs. Whereas DST investors are considered to have a direct ownership interest in the real estate owned by the DST because of the regulations adhered to by the DSTs. REITs do not operate under these same regulations and therefore, their investors do not maintain a direct interest in the real estate owned by the REIT. As a result, REIT investments cannot qualify as eligible properties that can be engaged in a tax-deferred 1031 exchange.

If your intention as a real estate investor is to create an opportunity to exchange property and defer capital gains taxes, REITs are not an applicable investment option. If you like the REIT structure but are looking for a 1031 exchange-eligible investment, DSTs are your answer.

Receiving many of the same benefits as REIT investors, DST investors:

- Receive distributions for all income earned by the fund,

- Do not have deeded title to the real estate and, therefore, have limited liability for the real estate,

- Do not have to disclose personal information for consideration by the lender,

- Are not responsible for making operating decisions,

- Are not responsible for managing the real estate, and

- Purchase shares as a security.

TICs

During the 1990s and early 2000s, most 1031 exchange investors who exchanged properties for partial ownership in large, high-valued replacement properties participated in the Tenant-In-Common (TIC) structure. In contrast to a DST, each TIC investor had deeded title of the property. Though this was a popular investment model, it was not a convenient model and had many drawbacks for investors. After the recession of 2008, the popularity of this model decreased significantly because of these drawbacks, and a way was cleared for DSTs to become the new partial ownership structure of choice.

Avoiding many of these TIC drawbacks, DSTs:

- **Do not require unanimous owner approval.** Perhaps the most significant advantage of a DST structure is that the unanimous approval of the individual owners (investors) is not required in order to deal with unexpected, adverse developments. This prevents delays in decision making and standstills when one investor fails to respond or rejects the proposed action.

- **Are less expensive and financed easier.** Another chief advantage of the DST structure is that the lender deals with the trust as the only borrower, making it easier and less expensive to obtain financing. For a TIC arrangement, the lender is required to approve up to 35 different borrowers. Because the loan is obtained by the DST, there is no need for the individual DST investors to be qualified, and their participation in the trust does not affect their credit rating.

- **Have no need to sign loan carve-outs.** Since the investor's only right with respect to the DST is to receive distributions, and they have no voting authority regarding the operation of the property, the investor fraud carve-outs are eliminated. The lender looks only to the sponsor/signatory trustee for these carve-outs from the non-recourse provisions of the loan.

- **Offer limited personal liability.** DST investors enjoy limited liability to their personal assets due to the bankruptcy-remote provision of the DST. This means that even in the event that the trust fails and goes into bankruptcy, the most that investors would likely lose is their investment in the trust. Any potential creditors of the trust, or the lender, would be limited by provisions in the trust and could not seek other assets of the investors. Therefore, no LLC entity is necessary to hold a DST investment.

- **Do not require investors to maintain an LLC.** In order to limit personal liability, TIC investors are required to maintain set up a single member LLC (Limited Liability Company) through which they invest in the TIC. This LLC can incur set-up, annual, and dissolution fees. DST investors do not have to maintain an LLC to protect their personal assets, and therefore do not have to pay state filing fees that would dilute cash flows.

- **Have no closing costs.** DST investors typically have no closing costs associated with the creation of a single member LLC as in a TIC offering, saving as much as $5000 per investment.

- **Have a lower minimum investment.** Because a private placement DST offering may have up to 499 investors (in contrast to the 35-investor maximum of a TIC), the minimum investment amounts of DST's are significantly lower. Most DST sponsors will set arbitrary minimum investment levels to limit the number of investors to a manageable number, allowing cash investments as low as $25,000 and 1031 exchange investments at minimums of $100,000.

- **Do not have trustee term time limits.** The signatory trustee of the DST will generally be the sponsor of the private placement offering or one of its affiliates. Unlike a TIC deal, there is no one-year time limit on the trusteeship or the term of the property manager. This will give the lender comfort that the sponsor will have a continuing presence in operating the property.
- **Cannot be inadvertently terminated.** A DST also has a Delaware trustee (required by statute), so there is no worry that the trust will inadvertently terminate.

Using a DST as a Backup Plan

A tragic, yet all too familiar tale: Peter decided it was time to increase his investment potential. He planned to sell the 2-bedroom condo he had been renting for 10 years and purchase a triplex or fourplex through a 1031 exchange. In compliance with 1031 exchange regulations, he engaged a QI to handle the funds of the sale and the eventual acquisition of the replacement property. The condo sold for the anticipated price and the transaction went smoothly. Peter then had 45 days in his identification period to identify three potential replacement properties. He found two fourplexes and a triplex that he believed offered him the investment opportunity he desired. Before the 45-day deadline, he notified his QI of his intentions and began the process of acquiring the first property.

Due to competition for the first property and unforeseen circumstances with the second property, Peter was unable to close on either of his first two replacement property choices. By the time Peter knew the first two properties would not be options, there was not enough time remaining in the 180-day exchange period to acquire the third property. Peter had to cancel his exchange and pay the taxes on the capital gains he earned from the sale of the 2-bedroom condo. After paying taxes, Peter did not have the cash he had expected and could no longer afford a triplex, much less a fourplex, without obtaining a greater loan amount, which would then have decreased his income potential.

The reality of this tragic tale is avoidable.

DSTs offer 1031 exchange investors a potential insurance policy; a way to guarantee (as long as the DST is open) 100% of their exchange funds are invested in a replacement property rather than taxed for capital gains. You can put your insurance policy in place by identifying a property within a DST as your third potential replacement property during your identification period.

If you can't acquire your first two properties, a DST insurance policy provides an opportunity to purchase beneficial interests in the identified DST and satisfy the 1031 exchange requirements. Because interest in real estate owned by a DST can be acquired in as little as three days, you don't have to worry about not having enough time to acquire a third option. The short identification period deadline can inhibit your ability to identify a property you know for certain will complete the acquisition transaction. But when you have a DST identified (if there is still enough available in the DST) as a candidate replacement property, you have a backstop to ensure you have a property to acquire and can close your exchange transaction before it's too late.

Furthermore, a DST insurance policy can ensure you avoid boot.

Imagine you've sold your relinquished property for $200,000, but your replacement property will only cost $150,000 to acquire. The remaining $50,000 is considered boot and will become taxable unless you find a way to eliminate it. You could look for a second replacement property to acquire, but you may not have enough time within your 45-day identification period. Likewise, $50,000 may not be enough to purchase a worthwhile investment property. Since you probably aren't interested in investing additional funds out of your pocket in order to afford a property you would consider worthwhile, you might have to consider the tax consequences of $50,000 profit. Or, if you've put your insurance plan in place, you can invest the remainder in a DST.

Investing in real estate owned by a DST can be acquired for as little as $25,000, and you choose the amount you wish to invest. You can invest the exact amount necessary to avoid incurring boot on your 1031 exchange – not a penny more, not a penny less than you have allocated for your replacement property. With a DST insurance plan, you can ensure you use all of your exchange funds to acquire worthwhile, investment-grade real estate rather than paying capital gains taxes on boot.

With a DST insurance policy, you can sell your investment properties that have appreciated and lock in the profits without worrying. Don't put your 1031 exchange at risk; put a DST insurance policy in place.

Diversification

Whether you're new to investing or you're a career investor, you've been told and understand the importance of diversity within your portfolio. The higher percentage of your portfolio that is invested in one investment or one type of investment, the greater risk you have of experiencing a significant loss of capital. However, when your portfolio is diversified among many types of investments, the likelihood that each type will experience loss at the same time is low; therefore, your risk of capital loss is significantly decreased.

Perhaps the majority of your assets are tied up into one investment property. Maybe you've thought about selling your property so you could liquidate some of its value to reinvest into a diversified portfolio. You could complete a 1031 exchange to acquire a lower-valued property and pay taxes on the portion of boot that you've liquidated for diversification purposes.

What if you took advantage of tax-deferred 1031 exchange benefits? When you complete your 1031 exchange by acquiring two (or more) replacement properties, you are limiting your dependence on a single property to meet your investment goals.

Real estate is a broad investment category; it is not difficult to invest in diversified real estate. There are many different aspects of real estate to consider that will differentiate one property from another: the property's purpose, location, size, tenant, owner, manager, and more. By choosing different options from the different aspects of real estate, you can stack your deck for a lower-risk, diversified real estate portfolio. There's no right combination that will give you a guaranteed real estate success, but when you are invested in multiple properties that differ from one another, you have a good chance of maintaining positive cash flow overall. While some of the properties may experience times of lower income production, others will thrive.

Many understand this concept and would be interested in purchasing several properties to diversify their real estate portfolio, but to purchase multiple, worthwhile investment properties they would need a substantial amount of equity.

What if instead of purchasing entire, individually owned properties, you purchased portions of multiple properties owned by DSTs? Your cash could go a lot farther.

When you invest in a DST at a 1031 exchange minimum of $100,000, you acquire a direct interest in a percentage of investment-grade real estate and can afford to invest in a second or third property to diversify your portfolio with top-quality real estate.

PART 4: CONCLUSIONS

Damian Mills was encouraged by the realization that his mountain house was a 1031 exchange-eligible investment property.

By being able to reinvest the entire value of the home, he could begin earning income at a much higher rate than if he could only reinvest the equity. Real estate was a promising vehicle for his investments, but he couldn't spend time managing properties and maintain the hours required of him at work.

With DSTs he could leave the work to someone else and diversify sensibly. It would take time to re-establish his finances, but, with the past behind him, it was time to move forward.

After looking into DSTs, Harold Walker knew he had to talk to his wife. It was time to retire from real estate management and enjoy the savings the property had built up for him after all these years. After selling his duplex, he would complete a 1031 exchange, re-investing the value in a DST as his replacement property. Harold was going to enjoy his retirement. There would be no more early morning maintenance emergencies, no more arguments with demanding tenants, no more new-tenant interviews. Instead, he would enjoy his grandchildren, trips with his wife, and restful nights free from the dread of what the tenants would bring to his attention next.

Harold was also pleased to hear about the step-up in cost basis his heirs would inherit after he passed the investments along to them. As it was, he could leave the duplex to his children, and they could sell it and split what cash remained after the sale; he knew they couldn't all own it together and continue to receive its benefits. However, if he split his investment between multiple DSTs, he could leave individual DST investments for each child. In that case, his children would have the option to liquidate and take the cash, or they could remain invested in a management-free investment and continue to benefit from the income earned off of the full value of their inheritance. By completing a 1031 exchange into DSTs,

Harold would not only solve his immediate problem and continue to provide for his future, he could set up his children for a perpetual inheritance. If nothing else, he was sure that last benefit would be enough to convince his wife this would be a good move.

1031 Crowdfunding and You

#1 Real Estate Crowdfunding Platform for 1031 Exchanges*
We offer a turn-key solution for your 1031 exchange. The 45-day identification period can be a very stressful event. Our experienced team of securities and real estate professionals have created an online marketplace of fully-vetted, investment-grade real estate offerings. Our 3-step process makes for a simple and straightforward 1031 exchange.

1. **Browse our Marketplace of Properties.** Join the Crowd to view our state-of-the-art marketplace of 1031 eligible investment properties. Here you'll be provided with all the details and documents needed to assist in your due diligence.

2. **Complete all Paperwork Online.** Our expert representatives will walk you through each step of the process to ensure your 1031 exchange is completed correctly and efficiently.

3. **Close in as Little as 3-5 Days.** The properties we offer are already purchased, thus removing any closing risk. Most clients are able to close in as little as 3-5 days. Kick back and relax, your 1031 exchange is done.

For more information on DSTs and to learn more about how they may fit within your investment portfolio, please visit us online at **www.1031Crowdfunding.com** or call toll-free at **(844) 533-1031**.

https://www.therealestatecrowdfundingreview.com/1031crowdfundi ng-review-and-ranking

While the information provided above has been researched and is thought to be reasonable and accurate, it's important to understand that all investments, including real estate, are speculative in nature and involve substantial risk of loss. Additionally, private placements of securities are not publicly traded, are subject to holding period requirements, and are intended only for accredited investors who do not require a liquid investment.

Glossary

1031 Exchange: The sale or disposition of real estate or personal property (relinquished property) and the acquisition of like-kind real estate or personal property (replacement property) structured as a tax-deferred, like-kind exchange transaction pursuant to Section 1031 of the Internal Revenue Code and Section 1.1031 of the Treasury Regulations in order to defer Federal, and in most cases state, capital gain and depreciation recapture taxes.

Accredited Investor: A natural person who has individual net worth, or joint net worth with the person's spouse, that exceeds $1 million at the time of the purchase; a natural person with income exceeding $200,000 in each of the two most recent years or joint income with a spouse exceeding $300,000 for those years and a reasonable expectation of the same income level in the current year.

Accommodator: A term for a Qualified Intermediary or QI (see definition of QI below). An unrelated party (All States 1031) who participates in the tax-deferred, like-kind exchange to facilitate the disposition of the Exchanger's relinquished property and the acquisition of the Exchanger's replacement property. The Accommodator has no economic interest except for any compensation (our exchange fee) it may receive for acting as an Accommodator in facilitating the exchange as defined in Section 1031 of the Internal Revenue Code. The Accommodator is technically referred to as the Qualified Intermediary (QI), but can also be referred to as the Accommodator, Facilitator or Intermediary.

Adjusted Cost Basis: See definition of Basis below. Agent: An entity that acts on behalf of the taxpayer. A Qualified Intermediary cannot be your agent at the time of or during a tax-deferred, like-kind exchange. For 1031 Exchange purposes, an agent includes your employee, attorney, accountant or investment banker or real estate agent or broker within the two-year period prior to the transfer of your first relinquished property. An agency relationship does not exist with entities that offer Section 1031 Exchanges services or routine title, escrow, trust or financial services.
Adjusted Basis: The original basis plus any capital improvements that may have been made to the property less any depreciation taken. Subtract this matter from the selling price to calculate the amount of gain.

Asset Class: A category of investments that contain similar characteristics such as commercial office, retail or industrial properties.

Basis: The original purchase price of the property.

Boot: Cash and/or non-like-kind property received by the taxpayer in the exchange - includes, but not limited to, mortgage or debt relief.

Build-To-Suit Exchange: A tax-deferred, like-kind exchange whereby the Qualified Intermediary and/or Exchange Accommodation Titleholder acquires title and holds title to the replacement property on behalf of the Exchangor, during which time structures or improvements are constructed or installed on or within the replacement property. Also known as an Improvement Exchange.

Business Assets: Real property, tangible depreciable property, intangible property and other types of property contained or used in a business. Exchanging one business for another business is not permitted under IRS Section 1031. However, taxpayers may exchange business assets on an asset-by-asset basis, usually as part of a Mixed-Property (Multi-Asset) Exchange.

Capital Gain or Loss: The difference between the selling price of a piece of real estate or personal property and its Adjusted Cost Basis.
Capital Gain Tax: Tax levied by Federal and state governments on investments that are held for one year or more. Investments may include real estate, stocks, bonds, collectibles and tangible depreciable personal property.

Capital Improvements: For land or buildings, improvements (also known as capital improvements) are the expenses of permanently upgrading your property rather than maintaining or repairing it. Instead of taking a deduction for the cost of improvements in the year paid, you add the cost of the improvements to the basis of the property. If the property you improved is a building that is being depreciated, you must depreciate the improvements over the same useful life as the building.

Cash On Cash: A property's annual net cash flow divided by net investment, expressed as a percentage. For example, if the net cash flow from a property is $10,000, and the cash invested in the property is $100,000, then the Cash on Cash return is calculated to be 10% ($10,000/$100,000). Cash on Cash does not include property appreciation which is a non-cash flow item until the year of sale.

Collectibles: Personal property, such as baseball cards, coins, stamps, works of art and memorabilia, that is held for investment. Collectibles are exchangeable under IRS Code Section 1031. Collectibles are subject to a higher maximum capital gains tax (28% as of 1/1/04) than other capital assets which are subject to a maximum capital gain rate of 15%.

Commercial Mortgage Backed Securities (CMBS): Securities collateralized by loans on commercial real estate. Yield on the mortgages is passed through to the investors, less a service charge by the issuing organization.

Community Property: All property acquired by a husband and wife during their marriage. Each spouse has a right to an equal interest in the property. Gifts and inheritances received by an individual spouse during the marriage are treated as separate property. Property acquired by the spouse prior to marriage, property acquired with separate property or rents or profits generated from separate property are treated as separate property. Arizona, California, Idaho, Louisiana, Nevada, New Mexico, Texas, Washington, and Wisconsin are community property states.

Concurrent Exchange: A tax-deferred, like-kind exchange transaction whereby the disposition of the relinquished property and the acquisition of the replacement property close or transfer at the same time. A Concurrent Exchange is also referred to as a Simultaneous Exchange.

Constructive Receipt: Exercising control over your exchange funds or other property. Control over your exchange funds includes having money or property from the exchange credited to your bank account or property or funds reserved for you. Being in constructive receipt of exchange funds or property may result in the disallowance of the tax-deferred, like-kind exchange transaction thereby creating a taxable sale.

Deferred Exchange: The sale or disposition of real estate or personal property (relinquished property) and the acquisition of like-kind real estate or personal property (replacement property) structured as a tax-deferred, like-kind exchange transaction pursuant to Section 1031 of the Internal Revenue Code and Section 1.1031 of the Treasury Regulations in order to defer Federal, and in most cases state, capital gain and depreciation recapture taxes.

Delaware Statutory Trust (DST): The Delaware Statutory Trust, or DST, is a separate legal entity created as a trust under Delaware statutory law. The law permits a very flexible approach to the design and operation of these entities. The Internal Revenue Service issued a revenue procedure on July 20, 2004 regarding the use of DST's for the purchase of fractional interests in real property that would qualify as like-kind replacement property in conjunction with a tax-deferred like-kind exchange transaction. Unlike a Tenant in Common investors has no control and must be sold as a security. Lenders frequently prefer because they are dealing with only one entity, not a number of tenant in common owners.

Delayed Exchange: An exchange where the selling of the relinquished property and the purchase of the replacement property does not take place at the same time.

Depreciation: A reduction in value of property over the property's economic life.

Depreciation Recapture: The amount of gain resulting from the disposition of property that represents the recovery of depreciation expense that has been previously deducted on the Taxpayer's (Exchanger's) income tax returns.

Equity: The value of a person's ownership in real property or securities; the market value of a property or business, less any claims or liens on it.
Exchange Agreement: A written agreement between the Qualified Intermediary and Exchanger setting forth the Exchanger's intent to exchange relinquished property for replacement property, as well as the terms, conditions and responsibilities of each party pursuant to the tax-deferred, like-kind exchange transaction.

Exchange Period: The period of time during which the Exchanger must complete the acquisition of the replacement property(ies) in his or her tax-deferred, like-kind exchange transaction. The exchange period is 180 calendar days from the transfer of the Exchanger's first relinquished property, or the due date (including extensions) of the Exchanger's income tax return for the year in which the tax-deferred, like-kind exchange transaction took place, whichever is earlier, and is not extended due to holidays or weekends.

Exchangor/Exchanger: The Taxpayer who is completing the tax-deferred, like-kind exchange transaction. An Exchanger may be an individual, partnership, LLC, corporation, institution or business.

Excluded Property: The rules for like-kind exchanges do not apply to property held for personal use (such as homes, boats or cars); cash; stock in trade or other property held primarily for sale (such as inventories, raw materials and real estate held by dealers); stocks, bonds, notes or other securities or evidences of indebtedness (such as accounts receivable); partnership interests; certificates of trust or beneficial interest; choses in action.

Fair Market Value: The price at which property would change hands between a buyer and a seller, neither having to buy or sell, and both having reasonable knowledge of all necessary facts.
Fractional Interest: An undivided fractional interest or partial interest in property.

Identification Period: The period of time during which the Exchanger must identify potential replacement properties in his or her tax-deferred, like-kind exchange. The period is 45 calendar days from the transfer of the

Exchanger's relinquished property and is not extended due to holidays or weekends.

Intermediary: An unrelated party who participates in the tax-deferred, like-kind exchange to facilitate the disposition of the Exchanger's relinquished property and the acquisition of the Exchanger's replacement property. The Intermediary has no economic interest except for any compensation (exchange fee) it may receive for acting as an Intermediary in facilitating the exchange as defined in Section 1031 of the Internal Revenue Code. The Intermediary is technically referred to as the Qualified Intermediary (QI), but is also known as the Accommodator, Facilitator or Intermediary.

Internal Revenue Code 1031: Section 1031 of the Internal Revenue Code allows an Exchangor to defer his or her capital gain tax and depreciation recapture tax when he or she exchanges relinquished property for like-kind or like-class replacement property.

Improvement Exchange: A tax-deferred, like-kind exchange whereby the Qualified Intermediary and/or Exchange Accommodation Titleholder acquires title and holds title to the replacement property on behalf of Exchangor, during which time new or additional structures or improvements are constructed or installed on or within the replacement property. Also known as a Build-To-Suit exchange.

Like-Kind Exchange: The sale or disposition of real estate or personal property (relinquished property) and the acquisition of like-kind real estate or personal property (replacement property) structured as a tax-deferred, like-kind exchange transaction pursuant to Section 1031 of the Internal Revenue Code and Section 1.1031 of the Treasury Regulations in order to defer Federal, and in most cases state, capital gain and depreciation recapture taxes.

Like-Kind Property: Property that is exchangeable with another property. Refers to the nature or character of the property and not to its grade or quality. Real estate is like-kind to real estate.
Loan-To-Value (LTV):   The ratio of the amount of the loan to the value of the property. For example, if an investor put $200,000 down and placed a $800,000 loan on a $1,000,000 property the LTV would be 80% ($800,000/$100,000).

Mixed Property (Multi-Asset) Exchange: An exchange that contains different types of properties, such as depreciable tangible personal property, real property, and intangible personal property. In a Mixed Property Exchange, relinquished properties are segmented in like-kind groups and matched with corresponding like-kind groups of replacement properties.

(844) 533-1031

NNN Lease Investments: In its purest form (called a triple net lease or NNN lease), the tenant is responsible for all property management and repairs - including everything from paying the taxes to sweeping out the driveway to repairing the roof if needed. The only responsibility of the owner is to pay the mortgage on the property.

Partial Exchange: When an exchange entails receiving cash, excluded property and/or non-like-kind property and/or any net reduction in debt (mortgage relief) on the replacement property as well as an exchange of qualified, like-kind property. In the case of a partial exchange, tax liability would be incurred on the non-qualifying portion and capital gain deferred on the qualifying portion under IRS code Section 1031.

Personal Property Exchange: A tax-deferred transfer of personal property (relinquished property) for other personal property (replacement property) that are of like-kind or like-class to each other.
Principal Residence Exemption: Exclusion from capital gain tax on the sale of principal residence of $250,000 for individual taxpayers and $500,000 for couples, filing jointly, under IRS Code Section 121. Property must have been the principal residence of the taxpayer(s) 24 months out of the last 60 months. In the case of a dual use property, such as ranch, retail store, duplex or triplex, the taxpayer can defer taxes on the portion of the property used for business or investment under IRS Code Section 1031 and exclude capital gain on the portion used as the primary residence under Section 121.

Qualified Intermediary (QI): An unrelated party (All States 1031) who participates in the tax-deferred, like-kind exchange to facilitate the disposition of the Exchanger's relinquished property and the acquisition of the Exchanger's replacement property. The Qualified Intermediary has no economic interest except for any compensation (exchange fee) it may receive for facilitating the exchange as defined in Section 1031 of the Internal Revenue Code. The Qualified Intermediary is the correct technical reference pursuant to the Treasury Regulations, but the Qualified Intermediary is also known as the Accommodator, Facilitator or Intermediary.

Qualified Use: An Exchangor must intend to use the property in their trade or business, to hold the property for investment or to hold the property for income production in order to satisfy the qualified use test. Real Property: Land and buildings (improvements), including but not limited to homes, apartment buildings, shopping centers, commercial buildings, factories, condominiums, leases of 30-years or more, quarries and oil fields. All types of real property are exchangeable for all other types of real property. In general, state law determines what constitutes Real Property.

Real Estate Exchange: The sale or disposition of real estate (relinquished property) and the acquisition of like-kind real estate (replacement property) structured as a tax-deferred, like-kind exchange transaction pursuant to Section 1031 of the Internal Revenue Code and Section 1.1031 of the Treasury Regulations in order to defer Federal, and in most cases state, capital gain and depreciation recapture taxes. Related Person: Any person bearing a relationship to the Exchangor as described in Section 267(b) of the Internal Revenue Code. Related parties include family members (spouses, children, siblings, parents or grandparents but not aunts, uncles, cousins or ex-spouses) and a corporation in which you have more than a 50% ownership; or a partnership or two partnerships in which you directly or indirectly own more a 50% share of the capital or profits.

Relinquished Property: The property the owner will be selling in the exchange.

Replacement Property: The property to be received by the owner in the exchange.

Reverse Exchange: An exchange that occurs in reverse order of a forward exchange, as the replacement property is bought and held by the EAT and then the relinquished property is sold - OR - taxpayer can transfer title to the relinquished property to the EAT and simultaneously acquire the replacement property.

Securitization: Indirectly investing in real estate markets (for example, investments made collectively with pooled money or the use of investment packages/funds, such as mortgage-backed securities sold on the secondary financial market) as opposed to direct investments where investors own property or hold mortgages; a long-term trend that has had significant impact on real estate values. Nature of investment can create major risk if assets improperly categorized and bundled.

Simultaneous Exchange: A tax-deferred, like-kind exchange transaction whereby the disposition of the relinquished property and the acquisition of the replacement property close or transfer at the same time. A Simultaneous Exchange is also referred to as a Concurrent Exchange.

Starker Exchange: Another common name for the tax-deferred, like-kind exchange transaction based on a court decision that was handed down (Starker vs. Commissioner) in 1979. The Ninth Circuit Court of Appeals eventually agreed with Starker that its delayed tax-deferred, like-kind exchange transaction did in fact constitute a valid exchange pursuant to Section 1031 of the Internal Revenue Code. This ruling set the precedent for our current day delayed exchange structures.

Tax-Deferral: The postponement of taxes to a later year, usually by recognizing income or a gain at a later time. Tax-deferred, like-kind exchange transactions are a common method of deferring capital gain and depreciation recapture taxes.

Tax-Deferred Exchange: The sale or disposition of real estate or personal property (relinquished property) and the acquisition of like-kind real estate or personal property (replacement property) structured as a tax-deferred, like-kind exchange transaction pursuant to Section 1031 of the Internal Revenue Code and Section 1.1031 of the Treasury Regulations in order to defer Federal, and in most cases state, capital gain and depreciation recapture taxes.

Tenancy-In-Common Interest (Co-Tenancy): A separate, undivided fractional interest in property. A tenancy-in-common interest is made up of two or more individuals, who have equal rights of possession. Co-tenants' interests may be equal or unequal and may be created at different times and through the use of different conveyances. Each co-tenant has the right to dispose of or encumber his or her interest without the agreement of the other co-tenants. He or she cannot, however, encumber the entire property without the consent of all of the co-tenants. In an Internal Revenue Code Section 1031 Exchange, an exchangor may acquire a tenancy-in-common interest with one or more other investors, as his or her like-kind replacement property. For purposes of Internal Revenue Code Section 1031 Exchanges, a co-tenancy must only engage in investment activities, including supporting services that would typically accompany the investment. Co-tenants that are engaging in separate business activities are treated as partnerships by the I.R.S. Titleholder: The entity that owns/holds title to property. In an Internal Revenue Code Section 1031 Exchange, the titleholder of the relinquished property must generally be the same as the titleholder of the replacement property. If a taxpayer dies prior to the acquisition of the replacement property, his or her estate may complete the exchange. When the acquisition and disposition entities bear the same taxpayer identification numbers, such as disregarded entities (single-member LLCs and Revocable Living Trusts), the exchange usually qualifies.

Three Property Rule: Up to three properties may be identified without regard to their fair market value. The Taxpayer may choose to purchase any number of the identified properties.
The 200% Rule: More than three properties may be identified as long as their total fair market value does not exceed 200 percent of the selling price of the relinquished property.

The 95% Rule: Any number of properties may be identified as long as the Taxpayer purchases 95 percent of the fair market value of all properties.

UPREIT: Stands for Umbrella Partnership REIT. Allows exchange of investment property for shares of a Real Estate Trust (REIT). Investment property is contributed into a REIT in exchange for shares of stock pursuant to Section 721 of the Internal Revenue Code. Taxes paid on sale of stock with no further tax deferred 1031 exchanges allowed. Non institutional investors can do a 1031 Exchange into tenant-in-common institutional grade property that may later be traded for REIT stock. Advantages can be greater liquidity and diversification; disadvantages include being subject to stock-market whims, not just property performance.

Yield: The return on an investment or the amount of profit, stated as a percentage of the amount invested; the rate of return. Yield refers to the effective annual amount of income that is being accrued on an investment. The yield on income property is the ratio of the annual net income from the property to the cost or market value of the property. There are going-in, free and clear, cash on cash and in place vs. stabilized yields.